Wren Blooms

SUMMI SINHA

Copyright © Summi Sinha 2022
All Rights Reserved.

ISBN 979-8-88749-907-9

This book has been published with all efforts taken to make the material error-free after the consent of the author. However, the author and the publisher do not assume and hereby disclaim any liability to any party for any loss, damage, or disruption caused by errors or omissions, whether such errors or omissions result from negligence, accident, or any other cause.

While every effort has been made to avoid any mistake or omission, this publication is being sold on the condition and understanding that neither the author nor the publishers or printers would be liable in any manner to any person by reason of any mistake or omission in this publication or for any action taken or omitted to be taken or advice rendered or accepted on the basis of this work. For any defect in printing or binding the publishers will be liable only to replace the defective copy by another copy of this work then available.

Dedication

Like many of us who have lost their parents and miss their presence in each moment, I too miss my father whom I lost last year and my heart bleeds when I think he is not with us anymore. I know how happy he would have been, and I share this moment with him. Whatever I am today is because of his grace. I dedicate this book to my dearest father who still walks with me in my heart and soul. Love you, papa.

I also dedicate my book to all my dear family and dear friends who had been a part of my soulful journey. Thank you all for being a part of me.

Read my book and love it and mail me at summisinha15@gmail.com

Contents

I Lived in the Woods Once Upon a Time!

There is no heaven
No hell
Here I am at the behest of time.

I now bask in the sun
Plumage of a tropical bird
I fly high.
A century later,
I will dwell in another time
Dining with the snow,
in continents, in temperate
near poles
I have seen birds from all regions
from time to time
I now have to decide
Who am I?
Lest I go wild
I lived in the woods
Once upon a time!!

I Offer my Poetry to Thee, my Roses

How frail is my rose
Yet her sinew of iron!
Benevolent, kind
what patronage for the bees she has
Repose in bliss
My prose, my poetry
I offer thee, my writings!
Enclosed within her
stings, bows in her bosom
her torso sieved
still resilient, forgiving,
she offered her honey
to the cunning folks
with all the dignity
and a knowledge that they
had come for her amber honey.
She gave them a name
Lover insane!
And they flew back home

forgetting which rose they robbed,

moving to another rose

without asking her name

or an empty promise to ever meet someday in

eternity

as if she never existed.

Insane were the bees

What bliss in treachery they have!

and I compose a poetry

A psalm of love

In honour of thee,

My serene rose!

Wren Blooms

On my windowsill
Among morning mist
A little wren trills!
songs of eternity
Hopping with her tender limbs
each morning when I hear her trill
A little bloom
above my nape springs
In colours of crepe
A Sufi song of meditation
In dervish swirl
my idea spins
and from nowhere
a little poetry comes
I owe my poetry
to my little wrens,
My inspiration, my muse
And hence the name comes
Wren blooms for my poetry book!

Sloted was I

From the silence inside
unto the chaos outside
Travelling a million miles
What tough a terrain
travelled it was I
Imposter life
never wants me to lie
Someone ground me inside,
or pluck me outside
What pain,
Behold!! My sky
The chrysalis knew,
he had flights untold
How meek are my kites
limited in flights
Slotted was I
Like her, between the edges of life!

Let me Stich Time Today!

Prithee, my thee
Permit me the dare to stitch time
My armour, my thimble I wear
Sitting behind the willow time
I thought I will today stitch time
A stitch in time
saves nine
Told my granny,
long time aback
uncanny I had felt that time but
today
mustering courage
sauntering through the memory lane
My first slit of time
was easy to stitch
A loss of my darling teddy
a soft twitch
on the wrist of time
A simple running stich
was all I need to do

and from beyond the mist
my teddy still smiles!!

Teenage was a time
broken and glued was it
so many times
Enjoying the bliss
I see there was no need to stitch time
some things are beautiful even when they are
ripped
a little heart stitch
in honour of my adolescence ditches
and the glitch was sorted out,
without a hitch!

Into the mid-twenties
time was torn apart
among family and friends
A young bride,
a swan
I wade through the trying times
My pinion drowned, swimming the ocean tide,
Leaving my bevy
was a heavy time

I was stuck in hedge
trying to pull out time
I failed so many times
stitching it was impossible
Ragged time, tattered I
some frayed times never mend
stitching a back stitch
bringing the seams together was so difficult
I found
back and forth, how hard I try
seams never wanted to be sewn, I thought
bleeding joints, I leave them unstitched
left it as it is
I took a new silk cloth and a pound of love
to fetch a new frock for my ol'e time
gave it a new design, a new perspective
and started life afresh
And moved on with the beautiful patchwork
I just completed
into the synapse of my mind...

My Rhett Butler, Why do I Meet You Again and Again?

I travelled westwards
To meet a man in black vest.
A thick cigar toasted his lips,
covered with thin moustache.
I fall for him,
I think, I know his trillion cells
He is my Rhett Butler with whom I lived in
century 17th,
in one of his versions' best
My pounding heart almost collapsed,
the flutter too heavy to stop
I ran to him and asked
Are you my Rhett Butler who lived once upon
a time,
and with whom I romanced,
your Scarlett in corset and laces,
and Margaret Mitchell penned
Gone with the wind,
in honour of us.
Are you real?

Or a wild fantasy, as many say,
that hit my nut into a gyre maze!
He stared at me as if my mind derailed.
At the moment of ecstasy, he told me,
Butler lived a century or two ago
Come in reality
Ordered he
tearfully I had asked "where shall I go"
Frankly my dear, "I don't give a damn",
and he moved away, this way
the million times I meet him
and the infatuation never seems to end!!!

Perfectly Imperfect

How do you define perfection?
A ten on ten
but who's ten
here I ask again?
How can I surrender to someone's else
definition
I am different
why can't you understand?
I am Eliza Doolittle
with a cockney accent
don't you change my chords, Mr. Higgins
I have different aspirations.
slot me not into
inverted commas of your fixations.

My aprons are all dirty,
my stew burnt
My cufflinks go into the soup first
before they land my mouth
my heels a patchwork of needle work
My foot full of corns,

thorns of wayside fern
The shape of my ankle awfully designed
as if a worn shoe,
just back from the cobbler's mend
My nail paints peel off before
I put them all,
my frizz hair so often I forget to gel,
my corsets feel so tight,
I am out of breath,
I yell at them and throw them out
With haute couture and heels high,
I fall like a house of cards
and I mess each time you want me
to be a perfect ten
I walk in with casuals and a tote bag
and minus the overdone doll face,
as you had asked
Eyebrows raised, buzzing rumours
my perfection scrutinized
The crinkle of the crystals, my head spins,
a sound of a broken mind
and I feel nauseated at the drama
of high life.

Into my tote bag, I carry things,
you will laugh
Dreams that the waves throw at me
each day when I walk on the beach,
A palette of colours,
that I steal each day from my butterflies,
when they were fast asleep
My little snail with whom I play,
hide and seek when I pat his hunchback
I grew up with lantana and weeds,
which you could hardly spell
I sneer at clouds and they shout back at me,
with their crooked tongue
and together we dance in the shimmer of rain!

A wildflower of your backyard, rustic and
uncultivated,
how can I decorate the foyer
A free soul,
plague me not with your norms,
the do's the don'ts,
conformation I abhor
Let me be,
with all the imperfections

O' the Pygmalion's of this world
Don't you carve me and
cut, copy, paste someone else into me
I am no illusion
I am a reality
Accept me the way I am
I have been designed by a Superman
Don't you try to redesign me
again and again

Oh! My Butterfly so Exotic Your Design!

O' my butterfly,
where do you fly?
I chase you
and you betray me and fly into the unknown
my wild gaze ends in a blind haze,
into a secret obscure dwelling you land,
where only angels play,
with gowns and bonnets of million shades
that they borrow from you each day
My lover, one day,
take me to one of your untold flights!

Is that heaven where you go,
after you
say goodbye to flights,
Unpacking your wings
you finally take some rest.

Who is the master who crafted you
Give that hand into mine
I want to kiss it tonight
How tiny is the human brain
So exotic your design!

Does your home
has a name plate?
engraved in gold is your name
Knocking at your door
I do want to come one day
Heads low
in honour of my butterfly!

Call me to dine with you in one of the parties,
you throw
I would rather be in your company
than a royal guest of monarchy,
so limited in flights and timid in possessions
I will take you one day
to my home
and show
How miser life has been
in throwing colours at me

It has been black and white
since long
I though love colours
And I love you too
blessed with colours of sky!!

The Colours of Evening Sky!

Whistle blows,

Off they go,

a race begins

clock had stuck five

twilight comes in!

Collars high

referee he is called

Orange shouts let me be first

Crimson grabbed him aside

How can he be left behind

shouted "I am first"

Yellow grins, some sunshine left, take me,
please!

Purple runs for her lifetime show

as if there is no tomorrow

slips, her bucket splashes

all over the place, she chatters

Jealous Magenta throws a bucket of herself

smudging the race I tell

Mayhem in the sky, chaos all around

Pink was sleeping
hurried too
Violets straight from bed
came in nude
let me run too!
Turquoise was quiet
silently moved in too

O' The colours of the evening sky
All of you have won!
Sky is overwhelmed!
Let her crown you all, one by one,
before it's dark and rivals come in!
Smudging the sky, black will come and spoil
the show
Hurry up before it's dark and dull!

Hold On!!!

Zephyr
hold on!
Wick burning fast
Put some oil
Blow soft
Until,
She spares her will to her kids
Her bun is in the oven
About to burn
Let her put it out
and glaze
Her little boy loves her glazed cake
Hold on till she gels her hair
Jasmine around her mane
Let her sleep for a while
Some dreams to stick around
Let her clean her wardrobe
And make some spaces
For the new one to peep in

In her hammock let her breathe
Beetles songs played on
Earphone sucked in
With a mug of coffee in her hand
She wants to live here some more time
It's too early for her to go
Spare her some breath
Until then zephyr hold on!!

Corridors of Eternity

A little rose,
that you left,
silently on my breast,
a tear here and there, enclosed within,
hiding pain underneath
You left me, saying adieu
came with me abreast.
Afterlife it travelled with me
Awake it was
when I was dead
They sang a song of goodbye to me
en route to the other world
Crooning lullabies
The journey was at ease
I take that little rose
and those tears hiding beneath it
A gift of love
From the corridors of eternity!!

Secrets of Universe Majestic

I stand beside the distilled brook
It ran to kiss my foot,
a foot fetish he has
A pink hue with curvy twist sailed my way
soft breeze paving its way
Below the sod dreams run
as your finger run into my hair
The hanging blue hue
Came dazzling too
The sound of nature,
the breeze plays
Flute atop a tree
to blow the trumpet of thee
A mail from thee to share,
breathless I did wait
Discreet they were
never to share
in their bosom hides
Secrets majestic!

Undressing the Hill is a Mammoth Task

Autumn came with a broom
Cleaning the mountain top
Undressing the hill
Crooked is the crest
Undraping the frocks
The hem came out
Torn side slit
I put a net on
How resilient I am
Undressing the hill
Is a mammoth task!!

A Special day in my Life

A special day in my life begins with a
fried sun
With salt and pepper,
my rain and clouds,
sieving from the sky
A glass of snow
with oak saffron strings,
My cutlery is all-star studded
A rafter from the sky,
and the table is all mine
Come and sit with me, Robert
and dine with me tonight!!!

June is a Funny Man

Zephyr, the sough,
sits on a bough,
lazily yawning
Chaos in the city,
the breeze forgot to blow
His body ached
and the doctors advised him a rest day

Beat the heat
Columns in his honour
Grandma's recipe for heat
Cucumbers and mint
to be dispersed free.

On my couch I lay
with June holding my hand
He is a funny man
stories of heat we share
Winking at the frustrating hours

June tells me,
he has summer solstice in the drawer
longest hour in the clover
Noon of summer, a bower but unaware
men and women fumed at this hour
not attuned they perspire.

But June and I
enjoying the noon
Draping the heat
enjoyed the frustrating hour with
mojito and mint
with some lemon rinds drowned into it
whistling a ditty song
Deliciously sumptuous are the noon
in the month of June!!

Nature is a Tired Man Today

Repose in her arms,
she sleeps peacefully
Giant nature is tired today
My wren sat on a dull bough
unhappy she looks
reluctant to sing,
Perhaps he had a fight
She is not ready to confide.

Roses are pale,
out on a bail,
someone plucked them for sale
The breeze is still,
Reluctant to blow, he keeps to himself,
inside his cocoon
snoring in his bed
'Do not disturb' tagged on his door
He is fast asleep
fingers on your lisp!

Sage butterflies
Kept their tired wings on shelf,
no more flights today they had announced
Moving into their rooms,
buzzing sounds make them hard to sleep,
they almost choked.
Drunk bees fainted on my feet
Puking honey they had cheated
fainted on my feet

Fire flames red in angst
Someone stole the apple he wanted to have
Beetles too felt sad
relaxing in the farmhouse they switched on
the radio
plucked in earphones
listening 'Julia' by Beatles
Wondering who was the thief,
who stole her silken stole!
Offence serious they announced!

My little pansies fled away
Into the dust some unkind say
Promised never to come back
Deep was her slumber!

Only God knows
what is wrong with her.

Cuckoo took a day off
He had a sore throat
singing all day long
My sparrows bloated
they had a heavy lunch,
off they go for a nap,
a rip van winkle sleep
in my lap

Violets stayed away too
silently into their zone, below their leaves,
sometimes in the ground

Baked sun
someone ate them today
Toasted on it,
before he can roast any
No syrup of maple,
someone stole it too.
Meetings going on
an FIR lodged!
My path covered with leaves,

heavy was the tread
filtered rain came in, very few to count upon
my skin feels dry, when will the rains arrive?

The ants finally decided to learn maths
They felt bored too
It was a dull day for them
lazily they sit at home,
and finish their homework, they abhor

I am in my bed
The Sun hasn't arrived to wake me up
My sweet cuckoo failed to reply
The cockerels forgot to remind me
The sun has arrived
Buzzing bees enclosed within walls
who will bring honey for breakfast?
No pansies violets for my vase
It's a day
Hazy I call!
Chivalrous nature
isn't greeting me anymore
I am bored
I lay in bed and the solemn nature watches
me from afar!

Summi Sinha ❖ 39 ❖

Stop the Blooshed!!

Check and mate!
Right on target,
Shouted inmates,
of this little dome.
Yay, yippee, congo
Claps for victory
Eek, yikes
dumbfounded stands defeat!
In the agony of the hour
What exclamations we have!
Below this little canopy
Whom we call OURS!
in snob attire!

A gazillion of zygotes
innate monsters,
herd of chimera,
illusions to be blown,
boom into a supernova they go!
But stacks of victory and defeat they pile

Life is judged as a war, peace has lost her
definitions
Life on parole
What's wrong with the men of this tiny dome
a puzzle, heads in a gyre maze,
Solutions, solutions, demands
men in white attire!

Hands in prayers,
how can war be the driving power,
of this beautiful dome,
whose ceiling is adorned with the twinkling
stars
and the walls of green attire!

The horizon slowly staggered down,
Our sun slowly moves into his black hole
and what pride we hold in our soul
of deeds of inhuman attire!

You are a nobody in this universe
The galaxy has hardly heard of you,
Ask the cosmos,
his head turns in denial

ask the sky
under his canopy, you live
they know you not et' all!
You are a nobody, stop, bearers of pall
Stop the bloodshed!
and say no to crime
or else the sky will bleed to death
today in scarlet attire!

Now at Your Will!

She landed her fiftieth year
Kids abroad,
husband engrossed,
doors ajar,
Order, order
You are now at your will, free to live
a life imprisonment about to end,
closure of records,
on parole,
you are released
Suspension of services
on ground morals!
Go and live, as you wish
Je donna ma parole
She gives her word of honour and leave.
Out on her own
she wonders
Where to start?
She went for her passions,
Stitching, her eyes blind

Cooking, but for whom she ponders
"Diet," had said the doctor
prescription of medicines
Her blood ran fast
and sugar, made it tough
She loved halter necks
once upon a time
but no skin show,
was ordered by many, at that time of the
hour
She though tries to wear it now
her hemp neck shouts
Let me be behind bars!
She did try to match her foot, marching
with the world
It's a different space now, she feels
Computers, mobiles
Hashtag, social media
Mails, cursors, cap locks
not a word,
she understands
She shouts
"Not my cup of tea!"
The world spreads in front of her, gigantic
and she feels lost!

She now knows,
she was better behind the bars
Tie her feet, take her back
the world is big
but there is no place for her to fit in
put her in the bastille
Disclaimer announced, nobody's fault
No warrant, no arrest!
She surrenders before the world!
She has forgotten to fly nonetheless!
It's too late now to start!!!

Divine Code!!

An ivy moved up and up
With its curvy twists and turns,
until he crawls the crown,
clinging to his mother's wall
He hung on to the trunk till,
he was taller than her
and reached the top,
to befall all over again
back on the ground!
to his native surround.
The call of the shore to the lost waves in high
sea, come back
and the waves do come back to the native
recall,
in thrall of an eternal code

A divine design of zigzag sway,
moves up and down to tell
Hanging before me, a code of universe lays,
slowly unfolding before my eyes!

You stick on to something,

the grip gets strong

Wisdom of the moss to hang on to the

slippery wall

even when it was cold

so that he does not fail

and not fall

till it,

reaches the top

and then the realisation that the sky stares
down!

the horizon staggers down

and a downward trend always follows,

once at the pyramid top!

Read the secrets of the universe

and walk slow

after all we all have to come down!

Gravity pulls everything down!

And in the seed of success lies the fall!

I Know Where the Ripples Go

I know where ripples go
into the deepest trench of your soul.
Within the perimeter of your heart, it lies
that little spiral,
that began with a dot
and you chose to ignore,
stays there for a while, trivial you had thought.
A man of no definition into his own gravity,
it will die
but you were wrong
to the core,
it never died, dormant he lied, quiet
until a day,
you suddenly see him rise
that behemoth!
galloping with colossus puissance
now moving outwards
it now shows in your body
you feel low and down.
Limping, a broken-winged bird,
lost hope to ever fly,

lost lone lanes of heart,
into a humdrum you go.
Oh! man he just nailed you in
your coffin drawer
and now he takes you,
towards the deepest trench of
your broken soul.
The wreckage of sail, on a lone island, from
where no one ever comes back.
The small gash you ignored,
shined on the rim of the black hole
now a scar, hard to heal
spaghettification of body and soul.
Into the black hole, you go.
Scattered twigs
hard to gather.
The spirals, like winds, adamant to flow.
How long could the wick resist
with no oil left!
He tries to shine one more time.
with all his power
the last try of his life but
losing the battle, into an inert zone you go
and ripples take you to
NO RETURN POINT FOREVER!!

Lily I Be

How placid are my lilies
Placating thee!
Happy forgiving
It's me
Sailing through the day,
resurrecting from the grave
Docile but straight
Crest on the crown
Astir with life
Tender is she
Lily I may be!

Was that Me

Some days riddles
Some days a puzzle
Some days suspecting
Some days struggling
Some days juggling
Striving for the day
I lay down
Wondering
was that me?

Stand Still

Spying, the trees
Stand tall
not a whisper
in the woods now
Here came a tiger
Finger on your lips!
The trees whisper, sough of breeze
run for your lives
Hide below the sod
Unshod your feet
or he may come howling on!

A Spec of Light Inside

For every step I take outside
I take a giant leap inside
A stardust from across the sky
I travelled an infinite path.
The journey was a tough one
A caliginous sky hanging over me all along
opaque fog engulfing me
in the weirdest hours of my life
The tenebrosity sometimes was camouflaged
holding me, a hawser, some sunshine did tickle
inside

With the ifs and buts of life
and right and wrong,
I travelled a rugged terrain
but I made it an easy one,
with a harness that hooked me inside
In unison with my inner world,
a spec of tiny light,
that roars in the sky,

travelling outside,
in the ocean of thousand stars and thousand
skies,
my inner spec holds me upright
and I am Me
because of my inner strength
Keep the harness strong!

A Note of Thousand Regrets

Trade my bone
Trade my emotions
Until you write
a little note of
obituary
Walking alone
to my gravestone
With roses tied in red ribbon,
the way you once tied me,
broke too
how will you gather them now
A dirge song you will sing
Asking me to come back
kneeling before the dead me
leaving a note of thousand regrets
in tears for me,
Your love!

Woman is Her Name

Me and butterfly
We are both the same!
She goes through her metamorphosis
I through my pain
Out of the womb of pain
we both come out sane
Breaking our cocoon,
each day,
to fluttering heights,
tumbling we come down,
with the gravity of pain,
to break the cocoon again
Butterfly is her name
Woman, they say!!

Broken Heart is a Syndrome Real

Who broke the giant oak?
An arrow in his heart
Don't they know
Broken heart is a syndrome real!
A dart right inside their hearts
What pains in heart's falling apart
Ask the oak befallen on the barren ground!

Morning in my Lap

Astir leaves
The trunks still sleep
Nibbling squirrels
acorn full mouth
a naughty boy,
sitting on the treetop
Here comes the sun
in his lap
he takes him
runs to the ground
Stretching squinting
I see all
He orders me
come out
it's day!!
SMILE, he shouts!

No Lines, No Burrows, No 11s!

My mother always sits,
on a chair
of my living room
below a lampshade
Her face so clear to me underneath it
She has few words to say
I stare at her face
from the edge of my eyes
Debarred of emotions
she almost looks dead
I try hard to see a spec of line,
a burrow, any 11s there
in vain.
Any pain, any regret, any happiness
that lives in her face
the wavelengths are slowly becoming straight
and into silence it will go, I know
Debarred of emotions, she is dying
from her face

Papa left a year back
she lost her lines, her emotions
And never lived again!!
someone breaks the ice or thaw her face
before it's too late!

A Hermit in Seclude!!

Love is the sorest
Of all human aches!!!
Ancient as human race
Old as souls,
an ace
You fall,
and he is ever ready to axe!

Perceived by all,
in different ways
A face so dear to us
and men loved to walk the desolate lane
A mirage,
doomed for a pitiless fall
Pitcher of venom,
still, thirsty men in queues,
lined up to be doomed
A grave where only the dead call
and the bravest of brave fear to dwell.

He had warned men of all ages
A prohibitory order
Beware of me,
a recluse,
a hermit in seclude
Don't enter my cave
into my meditation, I don't like anybody
Put your foot forward,
and
off the cliff,
you will fall
But like zombies
we did follow the pied piper
and he smiled at us from afar,
victory flag in his hand
Smiling, he said
Didn't I warn you?
Not to intrude
In my solitude!!

My Cukoo Travels a Foreign Land

My cuckoo travelled abroad,
she thought
Came with lyrics and a band!
Hoardings of foreign land
and jingles no one understands
She forgot her native tongue
Ambitions, berserk her mind
Foreign ideas captured a local woman!
Trotting the globe, she thought,
Miles though betrayed her,
she had only travelled the adjoining land
Running with her tiny feet,
how far she could have gone
But wild was she
She moved around like a snob!
Jocund in the air,
as she started to sing,
leaves went up and up,
like mountains they rose
Barking birds on trees

and dogs flew by!
Wild was the ambience
Dancing was the crane
his funk style,
Hip hop
only he understands
Welcome, for the tourist returns,
The world went upside down
Hey! Behold the drama is still going on!

Who Put a Price Tag on My Smile?

Smiles are priceless
But somebody put a tag
It was abundant,
free as air
Robert, do you know
who kept it on the shelf?
and gave a barcode to it
Don't they know it's free of cost?
and time was not a bar
Without a fare,
it was available to all, any time of the hour

But
now I find few faces with a smile
It has become expensive
and fewer men afford it
Into the shopping malls,
men queue up
Smile is now a commodity scarce
and people shy away,

thinking it was beyond their pocket slot
Upon the Heaven's sky
smile was bestowed to us without a price
I though will walk bare
and not buy smile
After all, smile is the least
that I can expect out of my life!!

Dyslexia Met a Small Boy

A small boy
Thought words look funny,
they flew like birds
and moved beyond his comprehension,
before he could read any
He poked his nose into the classroom door,
until his eyes ran up the sky,
staring into it, he asked
Is there anyone
who can tell what alphabets are all about?
To him it looked like a work of art,
drawn on the classroom board with chalk
Who can decipher words for him?
How funny, he thought, and he spelt it all
wrong
Everyone thinks he is a fool
Roaming the school

He, though, can see what we can never see
And hear hertz far away from us, his neurons
are different
his wiring is different
and boys found it amusing

Until the day, dyslexia came to meet him in
his classroom
He thought he knew this man by heart
his childhood friend whom he had lost and
he knew him from the start
They are now friends and understand each
other so well
They cry and learn words
Until they fly by
to another world
Words don't live in their world after all!

An Ode to a Silent Lover, the Sunflower

O my flower of love!
Staring at the eastern sky
With a blush
along the crimson hue,
A blond lady,
undrapes her yellow skirt,
beneath, a brown corset she adores,
on her breast
Sweet with lark
She shows up and blossoms,
into love,
singing hymns of fidelity
and carols in praise of her thee
Her lord!

With an arrogance
The mighty moves in too
into the day,
with a bang

She sparkles into a young maiden
When he hovers overhead.

Prick of heat
Shouted men
and she whispered love,
in the ears of her lord.
Indifferent, he moves away
as if she never was.
He slowly moves down the stairs,
lands on the ocean floor
her eyes, mortal bound.

She withers with
a whimper, no one hears of her again
Singing a dirge song,
blooming with love,
eternal was she
Until her thee moved beyond,
into the unknown
she lost her being
Wilted, she died
staring at the eternal sky,
praying for her lover to rise again,
in the mortal eyes.

Madly in love
Lover of sun
My darling sunflower
what do you get?
You love his burn
the soothing moon did give you pain
My princess, my Cinderella,
he is not your man
Why do you love him?
Here, I ask again.

I get all, in loving Him
The way He loves all
Burning through the day,
dust and gale
Pastures and meadows,
hills and desserts
Sauntering for all
He forgets none
He is a true master I say
and I love Him the way He loves all
He is a messiah with a message strong
Love thy all
But don't you expect at all
And I learned it by heart!!

Winds are Smart

Spying, the forest
The wind blew unrest
Rafters of emerald
falls before me
Wind, the villain
spilled secrets disguised
Blowing with his gigantic arms
wand of magic, he plays out
Sparring swords, he wants everyone
to come out
Hidden Brooke came laughing aloud!
Muddling, the spring came out too
surrendered long before anyone
can find him out
Hue of amber, purple, scarlet
came in too
showed me the forest duff
and little ant surrendered too
Everything bared before him
Wind did remove the curtain green

Giving wind the credits and his due

Bow before Him

declared the forest, in respect

Wind is smart, he knows all

into the cart of forest

secrets unravelled part by part

Winds are mighty

they know how to get the secrets out!!!

Summer Solstice in
My Wardrobe Teal

I walk North
A bunch of birds,
in colourful socks and frocks
and bright sunshine,
sat on my city parapet
I ran with my breath few,
panting, my wardrobe ajar,
Birds flew away with my socks and frocks
and summer solstice I secretly hid last year
at this time of the hour.
Birds though clever than I thought, knew,
wheel of time turned around,
a year did pass,
birds came to steal,
my wardrobe teal
and they let my solstice free
from the Creel,
with so much noise of fun and frolic
Equality be the theme

I beam too
and let them dress in pretty frocks of me
Bees flew away with honey in bottles and jars
So much merriment all around
The maze now as simple as my roses
and the haze did clear away
The sun shines amber
in it is the wisdom of the earth!

Light the campfire
A feast hearty
After all you have
A long, long day to wear
Roll your sleeves up
Dance your heart out,
till you fall down
What a delight to find out
There is some more sunshine left,
in my left pocket slot
Oh! The pleasure of summer solstice
I want to hug my sun tight
and again, hide in my wardrobe teal
and throw away the keys
My Sun, don't you leave me tonight

in his lap I will sleep
Until summer solstice lands
in my lap after days three sixty-five
After all, we all know
The Sun will get miser now on
and who likes it anyhow!!!

Betrayal Called Rape

Her armour with a clatter broke,
she choked in her cloak
and time stood in silence
Witnessing a penance
A vow to be made
distrust, was echoing in the background
She was slayed by her own men
RAPE is the word
Betrayal, the keyword
INHUMAN echoed the universe!

Tropics

I am a little, little bird
A brittle, brittle soul
Abashed by snow
in a temperate zone
I moved down a few latitudes below
and what a show
Little, little birds
wore colourful stole
Strolling in the fresh breeze
basking below the sun
a rainbow hair band,
adorned their mane
Like a candy of vibgyor
in a baby hand
What a fun to see them run!

Stout was their souls
Merrier by the day
Content by the night

On the shiny grass of morning dew
they laid on a bedsheet of spring delight
and a promised I made to myself, never to
visit temperate again!

Take Away the Scaffolds

Scaffolds circled my home,
girdles my ribcage,
hardly I breathe
Blindfold I stand still
Air is scarce,
choked inside is me
An army of design,
longlegs came forth
captured my homes
Peons left the barren house
Winds monitored who came in
Who left by?
The caw of crow
I hear my calling bell ring
Bats hanged
My name plate topsy turvey
An aerial display
Boggled was my mind
Amazed by the maze

masquerade, my home
a haunted house it looked
And lo! in all the fuss
I forgot my house name
and knocked some other door!!

I will Dunk into Life, Toasting on it

One day
I will get drunk with life
and dunk into life odyssey
A magpie into the puddle of life
Drowned I will be happiest, I know

Beyond the glass houses
Where emotions and life are fragile
Fear begets fear is the theme
Murphy law working
Things happen as you anticipate
And life does break like crystals
Parrerall an open pathway of life exists,
unaware of what others say
Sleeping below the umbrella sky
abreast with life
Men move in enthusiasm and no fear at all
in little tea stalls
and buzzing hawker's zone and slum dwellings

I will walk with the unprivileged
and learn from them happiness
After all they know happiness best
in the miseries of life!

Titanic Finally Settled Down

Deep was the sea,
deeper was the drown
Early spring,
came a mayday scream
men in ties and boots,
maidens in crystals and golden hem
pearls assembled in the silver thread
broke down too
Settling on the seabed
They never got a chance to adore anyone again

Lovers embraced
They knew they will never meet
Promised to meet someday in eternity
The orchestra of death slowly played
Drumbeats like heartbeats
slowly withered away
Fumbled words of men and women,
shivered on the cool walls of the sea,
lost to eternity,
no one heard of them again.

But among the chaos
A secret order went on,
on the sea floor
They opened the tavern's door,
to offer the dead,
the best of wine, from vines
hanging on its walls
Mermaids dressed in scales of silk
Welcoming them with a welcome drink
Melancholic orchestra played,
for the galore before
A thanksgiving on the sea floor
Swimming with the shoals
they came spinning down,
they finally settled on the seabed
Rubble of yesteryears
into the water graveyard
laid in there
Titanic finally settled down!

Ageing Beautifully

I stand bare before a mirror
To see myself,
hanging on me was age
Pounds of flesh,
oodles of love that life gave me
Erupting lava bed
Love handles
outbursts of ginger
on a winter night,
Proud were my tyres
protruding, they smiled at me
Boobs did hang down
but it still has some shape and
some pride left, although
a willow tree,
a year or two
before it finally droops.
Gravity, the final call
finally pulling everything down!

I take the flattering of men
I have aged beautifully
Like a fluttering butterfly,
before her last flight
and
I see my body as a black hole
Lying in my own gravity
my soul shining,
before the last sleep.
An event horizon on the rim
before it sucks everything
The wick shines bright
After all, it was the last night!

Neighbours in Grave

We were neighbours in grave,
abutting together we stayed,
naked and discalced
they left us in our graves
and fled away
Below the stack we sat and cried
embracing each other's pain
Timelessness was our attire
aeons our destination
We cajoled ourselves
for the beetle sleep, hoping
the spring of eternity
will someday come.
A callout for us to be awake
Until then, rest in peace
a truce we made.

Jennifer told me she was very wanted
a walking elf,
stitching, baking, cooking stew,

she knew she will be missed each day
Every now and then
guests in tears
arrived at her grave
To pay silent tribute
bees humming, the pale roses
had finally no nectar to spare!

She would sneak out from her mossy curtain,
at midday or the night,
to welcome guests with candlelight
Tired and weary were her days
after all, she could hardly sleep,
in the mayhem at her grave!
Days were snappy as she arranged heaps of
flowers
that the guests left away in respect
She never really needed them
and one day she tumbled like an empty glass
about to break.
Furious at her plight
I called her aloud to tell
Listen babe!
Didn't they tell you to rest in peace
when they lowered you that day?

Didn't they cover you with handful of clay
forgetting you were human
stuck below the knoll of pain!
Don't they know even dead need their space
A power nap in the noon
some little 'my time' space
Struggling with the spatula and spoons
Don't they know, you can't cook a soulful meal
for yourself?
How selfish they can be
Crawling into your privacy
Aren't they scared of the eerie grave?
Or,
are they guilty of not taking care?
when you were with them all time of the day
Now tell them to stay away
'Do Not Disturb' placard to be
fixed near your grave!
After all you are in transit
and a new journey lies ahead
Till then, rest in peace
until life comes calling again!!!

Was this Religion Penned by Gods

In slogans
Roars words of God
Never penned by Him
Bullet, stone pelted
as if words kind
The hold on daggers got bold
Love whispered some Braveheart
to be slaughtered on the insane path
they bled
And men called it RELIGION!
Falter of ten commandments
A flaw called religion
Angst it shouted
Murder was the theme
Religion bled
Was that I?
and my teachings
mocked God!

Latitudes

I ran to the forty-fifth floor,
without a breath to take
and a jerk to feel
as if air has perks to pay,
through the velvety way.

Narrowing roads towards the top
Panting I reached the sixty-sixth floor
My heart pounded heavily and said a 'No' to
me
Foot heavy to unpluck, into the ice they froze
who stalled it, I ask, someone thaw it for me
The richness of the globe separated from
this floor
Ermines came forth on my skin,
bonnets around my chin
Words shivered like autumn leaves,
moaning, I had snow for dinner and lunch
Oh! How I miss the drench of my summer fun
I raised my head to have a glimpse of my sun

To plead him
Bake me once more
and tan like never before
but he was missing from the scene
Moving north up the poles
I had thought will be great fun
A bottomless pit,
of white graveyard,
it was so dark and dull
Miser is poles
sneered the latitudes of the Sun!
and I love the tropics even more!!

Does Immortality Lives on the Other Side of the Hill

Chasing the sun,
I run behind the hill
To see if immortality lives there
Does he have a face,
that I so long to wear here
Does he dress like me?
and live in a body,
so limited in space
Does gravity pull him down
Or,
breaking barriers of gravity,
into escape velocity,
roaring into the unknown
Is he a giver?
Or as miser as mortality
on this side of the hill

Is he soft spoken?
A wind soughs
or as lousy,
as my crooked clouds
bursting thunder into my ear rumbles inside
my heart any time of the day he wants
Insensitive like my bees
Sucking nectar without a fee
Or as sensitive as my Touch me not
Wilting in my arms
They tell all
anytime of the day that he wants!

Is he timid and frosted like my snow
or my colourful rainbows
that render my sky
each time that I fall
Can I bribe him with emeralds
rubies and pearls
or is he ample without a tag
Like my oxygen so abundant here
does he hold a price tag?

Limitless like my cuckoo flight
Or me caught between the edges of life
Is minting money is the only virtue he
knows or enchanting as my rose,
my swaying butterflies
Will it give me joy?
or just another passer-by
whom I sneered the other day
not knowing his price
Aren't there any among mortals who can
 tell me how immortality lives
I though choose mortality
Living eternally is not a bliss!!!

Scarlett have you Dressed in Red Tonight

The vermillion sky
Auburn tree!
A red robe on the shoulder falls
Oh! Scarlett have you dressed in red tonight?
or did your blushing on the horizon reflect
I saw myself in the mirror
of the sky
together we blushed with a crimson hue
Romance was on crest tonight!
Oh Robert, take me in your arms
Tonight, is the night of romance
run your fingers into my mane
till I am fast asleep
I am so tired
bless me with some love tonight!

Broken Hearts Bleeds Again

Broken heart
How can it be glued?
Any cobbler who can mend?
Any words that can soothe?
Any confession that can take the pain away
Will divine forgiveness ever be granted
Any song that comes to your mind
Can really silence the clatter
Try a thousand time
Fail a thousand time
Some ripped time never heals
Stich, a patchwork
Time will tear it again
And broken hearts will bleed again!!

My Cumbered Mind Slumbered in the Coziness of the Noon

Whilst the bright Sun shined on me,
in the glory of the world
My cumbered mind, did slumber
in the cosiness of the noon
Asunder,
whirlpools, gusty winds
flurried on the dark damp impoverished,
rim of my mind
Hibernating, it slept quiet on the duffs,
sewing my mind
Those camouflaging thoughts
below my canopy mind,
shrubs, dwarfs
maggots, a slimy climb
Guile vines and lianas,
now gigantic in form
walking on me,
now taller they can see
Strangulating I feel

a wicked wizard,
Rasputin you can call,
into the czarina mind
limping empire
smudging her mind
a mousse I will call.
An army of captivating thoughts
below the canopy mind
came to see me
in the silence of the hour
Strangers I know not et' all
Paint my canvas white
a demon might
Born on a poison night
and they had murmured
you are the one who nurtured me
all this while!!

Unlatch your Mind

Thou frozen soul
Latched behind the mind
Can you ever flow?
to the blue sea back home
Many a soul failed to yield
amidst a raging tempest
Braveheart wilted, wheeled into oblivion
long afore they fought the war
Bolted behind their minds
digging graves of selfish deed, until a knoll,
climbing they came down, a rolling stone,
into the graveyard back home
So, keep the door ajar
Let the song of universality play in
From a frozen mind, the sparkle of a beck
into a rivulet is born, into the blue sea back
to home.

Behind the ablaze of your eyes
Lives your consciousness divine
Forage the secrets

a universe outside
a universe inside
a biome outside
a biome inside
Move away from the domain of me and mine
To the domain of thee and thine!
From finite to infinite
And what bliss hither
Angels failed to define
A childlike bliss,
be it tempest or squall
This universe will never give you an
appreciation letter
you are none but all
The meanderings of the little earthworms,
the flickering lights at poles
The movement of celestial within its orbit
each working as the yclept nature
Mind is that enemy which breads
all pain and agony
Beyond the human mind, miracles do happen
esoteric life, which even the sweetest
nectar fails to comprehend!

Aristotle and Plato

Lyceum was a pilgrimage
I so wanted to make
To walk through the toughest terrane
To hear MY Thee speaking around the hedge
A wandering ecstasy in blood and vein,
and me
in his lighting presence
match up to a speed lightening,
putting down his ideas on paper and pen
How defined his facial lines
Enclosed in it, ideas divine
learning poetry at his behest
What a sublime era
Thou matcheth none
When Aristotle in blood and flesh
walked this planet of earth
Envious of men and women
who travelled the blue planet
when Aristotle Lyceum and Plato's Academy
parallel they ran
A mousse of ideas

Idealism of Plato
Practicality of Aristotle
Moved men
and when Alexander, a baby then,
was groomed under the master's pen!

When Plato called poets liars on earth
and Aristotle penned POETICS,
to entice men
To prove the poet's worth
Poetry was made in heaven
a mimesis of words
Poets live in fantasies, but their words are real
and who can tell you this better than the
master himself
A portrait real
A panacea for all
Be it philosophy, literature,
mathematics, or arts
He was a genius
embodied a world
Where Plato, his teacher, failed to live
After all idealism fails to sustain
in the reality of this world!!

Books Come to Meet
My Pages Though Precise

I read a book!
Over and over again
until the book said,
I am done for the day
My stomach did puke
Spooked book ran on the shelf,
promised never to come back again.

Stout was my body
I looked like words
No one seems to recognise me nor
understand me
when I stood silent on the shelf
Men and women see me in disdain
as if I was never a man
they perhaps thought I was a misfit
I tell them I am richer than they ever can
No diamonds and gold,
hanging from my lobe

In my dome,
lies an abundance
of an Angel's home
fathom they can never

Books come to meet me,
pages though precise
I meet my thee,
unseen from the naked eyes
I am richer in wisdom and wise,
as I complete my last read,
which money can never bargain
Books are made in heaven, where angels play
with words
and send mails to souls
in envelopes of love!

I am a book that walks and talks
With a hard cover
written on it my name
somewhere in between
Mirth my soul
searching you will come one day,
wondering how content anyone can be

Reading those lines
that was abandoned by time
and
orphaned by men
O! behoveth man loveth book like a beloved
Never will she betray
Thou name is book!

Pain be it or pleasure
nothing mows me now
I read a book last night
I walk like a giraffe
with my head sitting tall and high
I am a lover of books
and I read and read,
till I am drowned
and drunk till I faint
Simplicity on the throne
Modest is ME!

I was Cooking Stew and the World was Changing Around

In the kitchen,
I cooked stew
Kids were hungry
and the next day they had school
In the wee hours,
I hear sounds
not familiar, I thought
ignoring I slept,
A little while after I heard a wail,
it was panic, I felt
They tell it is siren,
and I had never heard it all my life

I had packed the tiffin
kids are ready in their uniform
but they say there is no school
I feel happy,
a rest day for me and the kids,
a sigh of relief and I sleep

But oddly
by noon
I am with men and women and children
Few I know
Influx breaking the barricade
chaos and silence together
a deadly presence
Below the ground,
Bunkers, what they call
Some I had met before
and thought they were happy
but I see them now, hapless
It's a war they say
but for what
I know not
Who declared it
Who are fighting
And for what
Who won
Who lost
I know not anyone
I was cooking stew in the kitchen
for my kids
and the world was changing all around

I Lost a Precious Day

I robbed myself today
Of treasures I so earn each day
Ate like a pig
saved the rest,
to wobble in the night again
Lying in the bed
clinomaniac, I say
promised not to sneak out
Books on my shelf,
Winking, they call out,
take me out, they shout
I ignored them outright
I failed to clean,
utensils in my sink,
water flowing out
choked drains yell it out
My bicycle asked me for a ride,
I tell them you go out alone
Forgotten chores
like granny's tale of lost and found

Nuzzling beer in one go,
burping aloud
they came out
choking my windpipe
I almost died
Drunk I stump the rat's hideout,
squeaking they came out,
they have to spend the night out
Chattering about me, the monster
that broke their house,
cursing they called the cat
I mew at them
Wondering they called the dogs
I barked at them
Ebbing myself so down
How will I come out
The day went upside down
cheating was I
Stumbling a day went by
A lost traveller's day lost
and it promised never to come back!

A Lassie Called Death

I heard it in family tales
and read about it in fairy-tale
Death is a forbidden fruit
An awe for all
but dare not any confess
It's midnight
I lay awake
besotted she lures me,
a scarlet dressed in red,
with blue frill hem.
I wonder how I would feel
When she finally arrives
one day
Will I be in awe?
Or
Will I whisper softly with the
hustle of the passing winds
that
I had loved her all my life

or will it consummate into a wild coitus
An orgasm of life
with the virgin lassie
called death!

Death is Omnipresent

The author of death is one and all
I saw it coming
to the kings in armour
to the knight with lance
and the pauper who was scared to fight
Author of death is no one
It was inscribed in the Bible, the Vedas, and
so many scriptures
Birth and death are twins
You are born with an expiry date
Declared at the back
A disclaimer for immortality!
CLEAR AND LOUD

My Abandoned Home

Maze of thoughts,
zigzag I ran after them,
time travelled fast
Hanging basket
An old sewing machine
O" granny,
you took so pride to own them
like a master does
Grandpa's worn punnet
with a torn velvety shawl,
under a trestle
of an old oak
limping it stood
fall of time.
Odours of lost time approached
smoked odours of charcoal
kiln burnt hickory smoke
overwhelmed I sat down
To open the treasure box

I put the keys
refraining, it stopped me
I broke the lock
impatient was I
A pinch I felt in my ears
twisting it was my Grandpa dear
With stern eyes
I though did not refrain as stacks of old
memories laid below!

Year 1980

Flapping the old dairy
Year was 1980
Writings were hard to read
a picture of teddy,
pasted in haste,
a mess
Time flew back bringing memories
like cotton balls
circling my old terrace walls
I do remember the picture,
granny had asked me to paste,
one day when you get to see it
you will realise how time flies away
Oh, granny how right and wise you were
to know my feelings forty years away!

My Orient Fan

Hanging roofs
My heart hanged too
hugging them was my old orient fan
I pushed the button and
Wow! Clattering it flew by!
Magic before my eyes
Some things never go wrong
old days stand tall
in the corridors of our hearts
I walk the littered floors,
memories prick my sole
nostalgic is my soul
Perfect as God
memories never go wrong

Time Travel into 1980s

Time travels back
Those words but perhaps lost
Hope though holds spirit
In a sunshine light
Shall I ever go back?
to the latched, lost home of mine?
Where dreams sat on the twigs of
mango trees
and slept on riverside
Meal was the lantana weed
when a python crawled next to me, and I
almost fainted falling on the ground,
scorpion into the shoes that I wore that day
stories of ghosts,
that never died
Oh, how I am stuck in those old days
Can anyone make a time machine for me?
a time travel I await
with my soul and heart!

Bliss is today Free of Cost

One day,
I saw bliss pass my lane
I sat in my veranda
and saw it pass by
Men in richness and rags,
followed him
like air
they had lost their definition,
yawp, bawling
insane, I thought
Bliss is free today
and what mayhem it caused!
Stampede, falling on chest,
fractured legs,
filling their bags with bliss
as if they have never met bliss before
Grabbed it
Toasting
The last supper
They still have greed left

Bliss though watched me
Sitting on my couch
I silently observed the chaos
Bliss asked me
Don't you want me?
I am today free of cost!
I replied I am ok without you,
on some odd days
waking endlessly in bliss
is not worthy at all
Bliss in singularity
it loses its glaze and charm
Come in duality
What bliss it has,
million bucks can't buy them!

Queen Bee

Oh, my queen bee
What arrogance in the bosom you hold
Swimming in a pool of honey,
drones and labours
slavery at your behest
Bring in more,
demijohns be filled
order of the day,
summons to be obeyed
or execution be the quest,
unrest be the theme.

Roses are pale,
yelling at their throat
leave me alone.
Marigold,
lustre of gold
sold away,
weary it felt.
It was a cold day,

shivering bees,
fold their wings,
holding their flight
they want to sleep.
In the hustle and bustle,
many of them land in the hospital bed,
foot plastered
heavy was the landing,
it broke their legs
Elves busy mending the broken wings

In the backyard
Cuckoo sing a
melancholic theme in the background
October theme played
but unmoved was the queen bee
more is what she wants
Inside the hive lived a greedy
queen bee in disguise!!!

How can I Stab My Pilgrim Meek

Pensive is my butterfly
He did mediate a night afore,
in the solitude of his heart
Betraying the roses,
an array of innocence
stinging the pink cheeks,
robbing her honey
What treachery in his bosom lives
He did think,
rendering him weak
kneeling before thee
asking Him "God can I"
bonded my hands
sewn my mouth
how can I stab my pilgrims meek
He though got a nod,
a pat to acknowledge that he can.
Nature had assigned the job to him and

he flies away with all the honey
filled in bottles and jars
And the roses wave them back
Telling him, 'Thank you sweetheart'!!

A Falling Leaf knows the Killer but Dare he Disclose it not

A little bird abashed in her flight
Down it comes a pouring rain,
from the sphere of air
falling effortlessly on the ground.
I hear cries of many,
in words, I fail to understand
I do understand,
there is chaos
The still soul,
encircled frost bitten many
around a campfire,
they dance and sing,
until they forget their pain
Was he a martyr or was he pained?

Unbroken his string,
moorings at bay
that still hooks many

Broken are they
who was the killer?
Restlessness in the brethren
questions left unanswered
A falling leaf came there,
he knew who the killer was
but dare not he disclose his name
Some secrets never to be unravelled
said a wise sage, with ashes on his forehead

Was he Vincent in Pain?

In the dingy Auver lane,
I met a local man,
in wine mane
ears insane,
in poorest of his days
I thought he was Vincent in pain
A big hello
I had said
and he moved away
Birched in pain
I asked the birds that perched on his
windowpane,
they told me
He was left on his own,
in Remy saint
Behind the smirched window,
he had watched the meadows
and lured to paint.,
Moved around the changing hues
with his easel and paint

The colours of hues,
a mask he glued
Behind those painful aches
of failing love
craving for it
Walking with his heavy boots
bares himself
in the month of June
Sitting behind the window bars
among insane pain
brushes went wild
and he dared to paint
His canvas white
with starry night
with the blues of his soul
whirlpools of his soul gloom
Perhaps impending doom
which will visit him soon
He painted the starry nights
with monsters of his insane mind
and shot himself
in the aisles of Auver

Honesty

Honesty is a lonely word
Eve teased and raped by many
He did try to befriend many
Few dared to accompany him
Asked the glittering dishonesty to
change its ways
Arrogantly he had said
I rule the world
Come in my sway
Honesty walked her way
It was grave
And the dishonest shovel dug honesty's grave!

Autism Doesn't Stop the World

A father and a son
Sit each day, at noon
near the windowsill of their living room
Feeding his adolescent child
they both talk in a language neither
understands
Love drooling
so, does words
Words crippled but
sounds vibrate
and messages do get exchanged
Eye to eye thousand messages pass by
Autism doesn't stop the world
nor the father or the son
They share and care
within the domain of their own world
and understand each other as no one does!

Battlefield Ajar

A cat and a dog
Played hide and seek from
behind a car
One peeps
and the other hides
War from afar
A mouse comes in between
and lo the battlefield ajar!
The trumpets blow, war declared
The cat ran after the mice
and the dog pounced on the cat
War announced
the mad chase begins!

Me, a Butterfly

The ringing bells of dawn
Rumbles before a storm
I, in the chrysalis,
a labour wild
a metamorphosis, a transition
about to happen
Behold,
the twilight sky!
a butterfly just flew
in a new dress,
was I!

I now lay in sky's lap
Gently combing my dishevelled hair
Knots of entanglements
Slowly weaning away!

Wondering Men of Battalion Ten

Parading came men
On streets,
in fleets
Trumpets blown; bugle played
and a Robert Burn song accompanied
Joy was the chief guest
a salute in honour of him
in the passing out parade
What a welcome for Joy, but,
Oh! boy, annoyed was Joy
attention demanded he not
He was a simple man,
carefree and free of cost
whistling the streets, he was a vagabond
but
men in streets,
eager in eyes,
low in voices,
stood tall and erect
An army deployed

lest Joy fled away,
was the fear of men
in mortal attire
Fists tight,
clasped inside was joy,
he was not allowed to break free

And then at the behest of sky
Shouted a man
in immortal attire
Stand at ease,
leave Joy as it is
he will be leased
barter with time
and Joy will be dispersed among all
Ordered the commander in voice stern...
Discipline please!

Joy all this while
Hated chaos
He was a blissful boy
slowly from below their feet
Joy fled away
After all he was a man of simple desires

Agape stood men
Wondering men of battalion ten
What wrong was done
Attention!, court martial ordered!

Men in galore, though forgot
Holding and arresting him, is not a way out
He is not a slave of any
Joy smiled from afar
chaos was what made him run!!

Life Left Me Behind

Life left me behind
I sat on a rock and
Saw it passing by

Song of puberty splashing around
Sprouts of doing, making ground
The dream to be a proud scout,
moved like a hurricane in my mind
To own a teal green shirt,
with badge of grit,
spewing bravery from the shiny edge
A necker around my tall neck
Oh! a dream so close to me
I had dreamed it day in and day out
no one deserved it more than I
Everyone knew bravery was my other name
A Joan of Arc in the make
and the day came but I could not make,
a bout of measles took my dreams away
Life left me behind

and I saw it passing by
Caged in the tulle corset
My bouncy bosom and tiny waist exploded
Walking through the eyelets was a silken lace
hunted from the dusty shops
sailing through the misty ways
Plucking in some stars and diamond
I got it tailored from the sky
The boast of Scarlett O Hara
of her seventeen-inch waist
to woo Wilkies
her mate!
and the psyche to smash her girdled ribcage
both went together hand in hand
and then the desire to woo
took the fear away
I shook, I jerked, I pushed
Finally, made my way,
to fit in it like soulmates
and looking at my zeal
Scarlett sighed away
But then my sister arrived
a plain Jane all say
leaving the corset and laces behind
Her refreshing condor

and simple ways,
took the young men's heart away
She walked in the limelight and
I stood aside
My pride a splutter of rain
hiding beside a wall I cried and cried
When life left me behind
and
I saw it passing by,

The oomph of the flavoured pages
Of Romeo and Juliet
Perhaps Shakespeare had penned me
I became Juliet and Romeo breathed me
How I wanted to read those similes of love
and metaphors of romance aloud
to make everyone feel the way I had
But I lost my passions
before the huge racks of favourites my
English teacher had
She had convinced me I write well but could
not read as well
Although no offence when I pen it now
I got to read it last
And the school end bell rang

And the romance had spilled in the
callous and hard-boiled reading
passing through the cold lips of the class
And life left me behind!

My lovelorn eyes
ineffable they were,
of passions desire and trust
I hid my propinquity
behind a pragmatic face
when I saw you with Julia in love!
I made a retreat
burying the trail
and gave it a name
Platonic love they say
and life left me behind

Me and My Mind

The house in which I stayed
Stood alone by the night
into a deep forest
Near a hill
A Bastille
Until Liberate Egalite Fraternite!
became the slogan of my soul's liberation
and Antonio had to be killed
Black and blind,
wild within
A ghost thought many
crickets screeched their throats out
lichens clung to my inner walls

Though I would confess
There is party sometimes
Halloween in the dark
Peak nose and a grief-stricken cane
walking, like a ghost I shout
Kids did peep into the keyhole,
scared

they ran for their lives,
panting the shared stories untold,
a ghost lived inside me
that nobody has ever seen

Until a fine morning
Amidst darkness spilled
I gathered myself
My courage and strength
And fled away from the Bastille
Liberated and free under the blue sky
I finally lived!

How Easy was the Hair Fall

Posting our bald heads
Contort distort we looked
Smirked we at our unconceivable look
Our buns removed
filters of fun
Heads grazed
what review of fun we made?
Little did we anticipate,
tomorrow is another day!,
confirming she had told us
she was about to lose all her hair
Our biggest fear
about to be true
Diagnosis of an aggressive cancer
she was brave enough to declare
Agape we all stood
a bunch of girls in late forties,
crawling stood the fifties
A fort hard to fall off,

how easy was the hair-fall
A day of fun was
ruined,
it spread fast
like our peals of laughter did yesterday!

Leonardo Defined

Superfetation of ideas
A splatter!
A sketch!
And the master chose definition
His brush had painted
a masterpiece
Depiction of mother and son
and he is born
of a virgin mother
Leonardo
blessed with her intentions to conceive
a hug of the divine on
the walls of her pristine womb
He tries to complete his imagination
but he left the masterpiece incomplete
He never knew how he got his other cell
He was never accepted
Was it a Don Juan wilt?

Your Life is Still Brewing, Taste it Once More

Why did you lose your way
On the behest of a storm
Your life is still brewing
Taste it once more
The beckoning of the shore,
to the waves at sea
come and kiss me once more
A lost traveller on a windy night
a frost-bitten inn,
a golden hem for him
And when the winter blues did arrive
you forgot to sing with the little robin blue
abreast of life,
this too shall pass
and the sunshine will land,
on the winter stinged cheeks of yours!

www.ingramcontent.com/pod-product-compliance
Lightning Source LLC
Chambersburg PA
CBHW021213130726

47988CB00002B/631